Teenage Information S<

Families

Ann Mitchell

Chambers

© Ann Mitchell 1987

Published by W & R Chambers Ltd, Edinburgh 1987

All rights reserved. No part of this publication may be reproduced or transmitted in any form or by any means, electronic or mechanical, including photocopying, recording or any information storage or retrieval system without prior permission, in writing, from the publisher.

British Library Cataloguing in Publication Data

Mitchell, Ann, *1922–*
    Families.—(Teenage information series)
    1. Family   2. Interpersonal relations
    I. Title   II. Series
    306.8'7   HQ734

ISBN 0 550 20567 5
ISBN 0 550 75220 X Students bk.

Illustrations by Hazel McGlashan

Printed by Eyre & Spottiswoode Ltd, Thanet Press, Margate

Contents

1. WHAT IS A FAMILY?   1

2. WHAT ARE FAMILIES FOR?   7

3. FAMILY CHANGES   21

4. ONE-PARENT FAMILIES   32

5. NEW FAMILIES   44

6. OTHER FAMILIES   49

1. What is a Family?

What is a family? That is a question to which there are a surprising number of answers. How would you answer it? Your answer would quite likely be a description of your own family, but there are many other kinds of family.

In any school class there might be a number of different answers to the question. Pam might say her family is 'my parents and my brother and me,' and Sharon 'my Mum and me', and Jim 'my Dad, my grandparents, my brother and me'. Lesley might answer 'my Mum, my stepfather, my sister and me', and Dick 'my Mum, my stepfather, my two stepsisters, my half-brother and me'. Michelle's family might be 'my granny, my uncle and aunt and me'. There are probably several kinds of family in your class.

Many people think that a family is two parents and their children, all living together in one household, but a family and a household are two different things.

Nuclear and extended families

Members of a family are related to each other by blood or by marriage. Usually they see quite a lot of each other and share at least some meals and some activities. A family of one or two parents and one or more children (and perhaps grandparents too), all living together, is called a nuclear family.

Sometimes it is useful to talk about an extended family, which includes grandparents, aunts, uncles and cousins of the nuclear family. They do not usually all live together, but they are related to each other.

Susan was talking about her nuclear family when she said 'my family lives in a small house with a garden' and 'my family has two dogs'. Ken meant his extended family when he said 'all the family come to our house for Christmas dinner'.

Sometimes it might not be clear which definition you were using. 'All my family is going to Mary's wedding' or 'everyone in my family is tall' could mean your nuclear family or your extended family.

Households

A household means all the people who live together under one roof. This might be a whole house, part of a house, a flat or even one room or a caravan. The people living there might not be related to each other: for instance, they might be a group of nurses or a landlady and several lodgers. Two families might live together in one household, like Jane and her parents who share a home with Jane's Mum's brother and his wife and their two children.

Only one third of British households has two parents with their own children who have not yet left school. There are almost as many households with a married couple alone. Some of these couples have grown-up children who have left home, and others have never had children, although some of those are young couples who are sometimes described as 'not having started a family yet'.

About a quarter of all households consists of one person living alone. Many of them are widowed and elderly. Some have members of their family who live somewhere else.

A family might be temporarily divided between different households. For instance, Tom spends summers on his uncle's farm and his sister Diana is a student: they each live in different households from their parents for part of the year, but they all belong to one family.

Parents in a family

Parents are usually married to each other. Some are not, either from choice or because one of them is married to someone else.

Expectations of marriage

Most people have some hopes and expectations of their marriage, which brings a change of social status. They get married because they love each other and want to live with each other. They can have romantic hopes of living happily ever after. Husbands and wives might expect to depend on each other financially after marriage and not on their own parents. They might hope to have their own home and to have children, although many couples never discuss that possibility before they get married.

Husbands and wives often bring different customs or habits from each of their original families. These might be quite simple, like drinking tea or coffee for breakfast, having a bath every day or once a week, which newspaper they prefer, which church they go to, going to bed late or early, or deciding whether to have holidays at home or away.

Peggy's Mum always dressed after breakfast before she got married, but Peggy's Dad was brought up to believe it is better to get washed and dressed before breakfast. Sam's Dad copies his own father in having a cold shower every morning. Peter's Mum was brought up in a family who often kissed each other and showed love and affection, but Peter's Dad had been taught that you should not show your feelings.

Perhaps you can think of ways in which your parents brought customs from your grandparents' homes.

Some families are very close-knit. That is, all the members are very involved in each other's lives. They all enjoy each other's company and they share many interests and activities. Other families are more independent of each other. Their members have separate interests but — as we will see in the next chapter — still need each other.

Two families

Some children have two families at the same time, if their mother and father do not live together, and are separated or divorced. Many adults have had two (or more) families — first themselves and their parents, then themselves and their children.

Other variations

There are yet more variations on the family, which will be discussed in later chapters.

Past history

In the middle of the last century, most families were bigger than they are today. Mothers had many more children then, partly because modern contraception was not available to them, and also because children became useful wage-earners at an early age. Then education became compulsory and gradually the school-leaving age was raised. That meant that young children were not allowed to go out to earn money for their families, so a big family was expensive to feed and clothe.

It was not uncommon for a mother to have up to ten children. More children were born then, but many died, so families were not necessarily larger than today. Sadly, many children died very young. They used to die from illnesses such as measles, scarlet fever, diphtheria and tuberculosis. There must have been a lot of sorrow and heartbreak. If you look at old gravestones, you will find details of families whose children died young.

And, of course, children lost a parent through death more often than nowadays. This was partly because of illnesses, with no modern cures, and partly because of mothers dying in childbirth.

Fewer children had grandparents then, let alone great-grandparents, because people were usually older when they married and also did not often live to an old age.

Family tree

Your family, of whatever kind, was originally formed by your two parents and your grandparents and your great-grandparents and so on. Try drawing a family tree, to see where everyone joins on. You could start like this, and see how many names you can fill in.

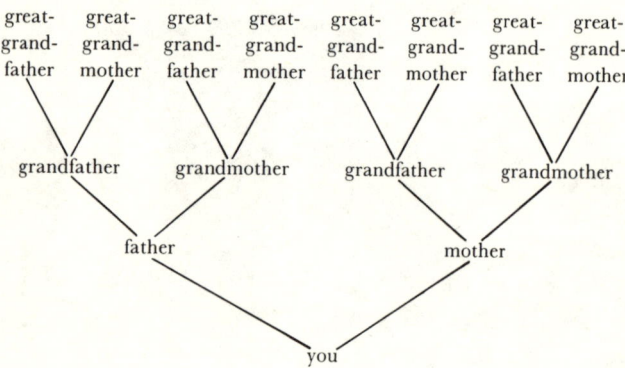

As well as names, you might like to add dates of birth and marriage — and perhaps of death. Perhaps you can add places of birth, marriage or death, occupations and also brothers and sisters.

A family tree can tell you a lot about yourself — where your family lived, what they did, how long they lived, what size families they had and so on.

Definition of a family

In this book, we will consider 'family' to mean the group of people who live together for most of the time, and are related to each other. So we can include members who are sometimes away working, or are in hospital or in prison or getting educated somewhere else. They share a home, some physical characteristics, some knowledge about each other, some privacy and habits and customs. . . .

2. What are Families for?

We usually take our families for granted, or at least those members who live with us. But it is worth wondering why you live together, and what advantages or disadvantages there are in belonging to a family.

What we inherit from our parents

You were born into a family and could not choose your parents. You inherited some characteristics from each of your parents. You might, for instance, have the same colour of hair as your father and the same shape of face as your mother. Some people look very like one parent — or even, strangely, like both parents at the same time. In addition, you might inherit skills from each parent, such as artistic ability, or cleverness with your hands, or a passion for reading or gardening or an inability to sing in tune.

Learning what to do in a family

From an early age, you learned how to behave from your parents, especially your mother. You copied what your parents did, in the way you fed, talked and got dressed. You learned from them what kind of behaviour was expected in the family.

Your parents taught you how to keep clean, how to use

a spoon or a cup, when to go to sleep or wake up. You found out what behaviour pleased your parents (such as obedience or helpfulness in fetching things), or displeased them (such as spilling food on the floor or breaking things). You learned discipline from them, so that good behaviour could be praised and bad behaviour criticised (or punished). You learned the difference between right and wrong.

Your parents may not have realised how much they were teaching you. Much of your early learning came from copying them, and doing what they did. For instance, you learned language from them. Small children learn the meaning of words, and how to use them, mainly from their parents.

As you grew older, people outside your family also had an influence on you — your friends or your teachers, for instance. But your parents provided models which lasted.

Characteristics of a family

What makes members of your family different from other people? Your friends are not part of your family, although they might almost seem to be if they spend a lot of time in your house.

Firstly, members of a family are dependent on each other for money. There might be one or more wage-earners, or there might be none. But usually one person has control over the money that comes into the home. And one person, not necessarily the same one, has control over how it is spent. The spending includes rent and rates, furnishing, heating, food and clothes. It may also include extras such as a car, pocket money, outings and holidays. So all the family depends for what they get on whoever decides how to use the money, as well as on the people who earn it.

Secondly, members of a family make up a social group. They can give each other love and companionship. People who share part of their daily lives may not agree about everything, but they are bound to have something in common and share the same standards. They don't need to explain the daily routine, or where things are, as they would have to explain to a stranger who came to the house.

Relationships

The members of a family might include one or two parents, and one or more children. The parents are (usually) husband and wife to each other, and mother and father to their children. The children are sons and daughters to their parents, and brothers and sisters to each other. So they usually have at least two different relationships, except where a single parent has only one child.

One person can be husband and father; another is daughter and sister. If there are grandparents or other relations living in the household, they will also be members of the family. Then one adult could be wife, mother, mother-in-law and grandmother, or brother, brother-in-law and uncle. A child could be grandson, son and brother.

Husbands' and wives' relationships

A husband and wife normally give each other love and companionship. They have a sexual relationship which makes them belong to each other in a very special way. They like each other enough to want to spend time together, and they feel comfortable in each other's company. They are usually of much the same age as each other. They share many of the same ideas about family life and living generally. They form a partnership. They depend on each other a lot and can give each other support when they are fed up after a bad day.

Children's relationships

A child's first relationships are within the family, with mother, father and brothers or sisters. These relationships are emotional, practical and economic in a way that later relationships outside the family are not. For instance, you can later be emotionally (but not economically) close to a friend. You will have an economic (but not emotional) relationship with an employer.

Children and parents

No two families are the same and in any family, no two relationships are the same. Parents often feel closer to one child than to others, although they may not want to say so.

The relationship between children and their parents seems to depend more on how they spend their time together than on the amount of time. Parents who spend a couple of hours playing and talking with their children will probably give and receive more enjoyment and love than parents who spend all day with their children but hardly bother to speak to them.

Children's relationships with their parents will change over time. As babies, they are entirely dependent on their parents. As they grow older, they gradually learn to look

after themselves. But parents will continue to influence their children, for instance, by choosing their clothes, their schools and where the family goes on holiday.

Then children start to influence their parents in turn. For instance, Marjorie could persuade her mother to try a new hair style, and Bill got his father interested in playing chess. Then, perhaps as teenagers, they sometimes rebel a bit. They want to make their own rules and life can be difficult for them and for their parents. The important thing is that their parents still provide a home and security. The parents are there when they are needed, but gradually they let their children grow up.

Children and money

At first, children have to depend on their parents for money and for everything that has to be paid for. Then they usually receive pocket money from their parents. Each family makes its own rules about pocket money — how much, how often, what it should cover, and whether some of it should be 'earned'. By handling their own money, children have their first experience of budgeting. Later on they may begin to earn money by working outside the home, and may give some back to their parents to help with the cost of running the home.

Brothers and sisters

Sometimes brothers and sisters get on really well with each other and like to do lots of things together, but they don't always get on well together. A child might get on better with one brother or sister than with another. Next year, perhaps their relationships change. As Betty grew older, for instance, she preferred the company of her older brother Fred (and his friends) to that of her younger sister Aileen. But she still enjoyed discussing clothes or having a giggle with Aileen.

In some families, brothers and sisters argue a lot, but that might be because they enjoy a good argument with someone they know well. Sometimes brothers and sisters just don't get on well together, but they often change as they grow older.

Older children often help in looking after brothers or sisters.

Roles and responsibilities

A family is like a jigsaw puzzle in which everyone has a place. Every member has a role (part) to play and has responsibilities within the family. Roles and responsibilities change over the years.

Husband and wife

The role of husband and wife is to support each other in every way — lovingly, practically and economically.

They share the responsibilities of the home and family. Usually he is the wage-earner (or breadwinner), though that is not always so. Possibly they both earn, in which case he probably earns more than she does. Possibly they are both unemployed, but still consider him to be the one who should bring in the money.

Parents

Most married couples have children, so that husbands and wives become fathers and mothers. Most parents have little or no training for a job which continues for twenty-four hours a day, seven days a week. They have to use their instincts and their common-sense, and perhaps remember what their own parents did.

Their roles as parents are to look after and bring up their children. They are loving, they give encouragement, and they provide models of behaviour, often without realising it. These models can be good or bad. For instance, a child will learn how to brush his teeth, tidy away his toys or invite a guest into the house, by copying his parents. However, he might also copy bad language or slovenly habits. If parents shout at, or hit, their children, the children will do the same to other people.

Parents provide rules and discipline. They don't allow a toddler to run out into the road, a young child to draw on the wallpaper or to use a sharp knife, or an older child to stay out all night. Discipline should be consistent and needs to make sense to the child. For instance, a smack (but never on the head) could be given for naughtiness but not if a child cries from tiredness.

A parent who tells a child 'don't do that', 'be quiet' or 'sit still' is being negative. A more positive approach would be to suggest some other activity for the child. That is, instead of 'don't tear up my newspaper' or 'don't make such a noise', a wise parent might say 'let's read a book together' or 'shall we play a game now or go for a walk?'

Parents have authority and they make rules for the family, about who does what, and when and how. These rules are not written down and may not be looked on as rules. But they include things like time (of meals, or bed-time) and space (who sits or sleeps where).

They share responsibility, not necessarily equally, for bringing up their children. They are legally responsible for providing a home and for seeing that their children are educated. They provide economic stability, security, love and happiness for their children. They share pride and joy, as well as some sorrow and disappointments.

Fathers and mothers

Usually, fathers continue to be the financial providers, and they take on responsibilities for providing housing, food and clothing for their children.

Mothers usually take on domestic responsibilities such

as cooking, washing and ironing, cleaning the house and looking after young children. Even if a mother goes out to work, she usually has all these domestic responsibilities too.

It used to be considered that a mother's place was in the home, looking after her children. Now, many mothers go out to work, often part-time. What matters is the quality of care which parents give to their children. Young children whose parents talk and play with them, or read or sing to them, will be better able to cope with life and school than children whose mothers stay at home all day, but don't talk to them.

Nowadays fathers are more involved with their children's lives than they used to be. A great many are present at the birth of their babies. Men do far more in the house than they used to do. This might be helping to look after children, or doing the shopping or washing up.

In a few families, the woman goes out to work while the man takes on the domestic work. This might be by choice or it might be because she can get a job and he can't.

Money

Husbands and wives have different ways of deciding how to manage their money. Sometimes the husband pays all the main bills (rent or mortgage, rates, gas and electricity) and gives his wife an allowance for housekeeping (food and clothes). Sometimes the husband makes arrangements for his wife to have the money to pay the bills. Sometimes they have joint responsibility.

Each couple decides how they will manage the family income. One or both of them will have knowledge of what their income is and of what bills to expect and when. They might budget very carefully, so that all bills can be paid. If they don't, they might find themselves unable to pay the rent, say, or the electricity bill. Or, if they live in poverty, they might have great difficulty in making the money stretch to pay all the bills.

Why do husbands and wives divide responsibility as they do? Is it tradition — doing what their own parents did? Or is it convenience, or male or female dominance, or pride? Sometimes the person who is the breadwinner feels some pride in having a source of power over other members of the family.

Children

Children have changing roles in a family, as they grow older. When they are babies, their unconscious role is to give pride and pleasure and to receive their parents' love. A baby soon learns, by smell, sound and feel, to recognise his mother and father. Very quickly babies learn to give pleasure consciously and also to give love with smiles and hugs. Isn't it nice how pleased people are, when babies smile at them?

Children gradually learn to do things for themselves, such as getting dressed or washed, or going to school alone. They learn to help their parents and perhaps they each have special responsibilities.

At first, 'helping' can actually not be a help. Think of three-year-old David 'helping' his father to wash the car, or four-year-old Susan 'helping' her mother to make a cake and then to wash up. Parents need patience and imagination as they teach their children new skills. Parents who continue to do things for their children, such as tying their shoe-laces or doing up their buttons, tidying up their toys or mending their bicycles are only delaying the children's steps to independence.

From the beginning small children can also cause frustration, anxiety and — sometimes — jealousy. An older brother or sister can be very jealous of a new baby who is seen as a rival for the parents' love and attention. Also, a father is sometimes jealous of a baby who takes up his wife's time.

The roles of children as brothers and sisters are to

provide love for each other, and to be playmates and companions. Often they share interests and secrets.

A team

Parents and children are a team. They live, work and play together. They can say things to each other which they might not say to someone outside the family. They can argue together and show affection to each other. They share experiences and activities. For instance, they go on holiday together or go out together at weekends or evenings. They know each other better than anyone else knows them.

Stereotypes

Often, roles of boys and girls are 'stereotyped' from an early age. Boys are given toy cars or trains, and girls are given dolls. Boys play at being cowboys or racing drivers. Girls play at being nurses or mothers. Even at school it is often assumed that boys will learn carpentry and girls will do typing or cooking. Boys are often expected to be better than girls at science or computers. Stereotypes like these can often be unfair to boys and girls who would prefer to have more choice.

Similarly, there are expectations about the way that boys or girls will behave. Boys are expected to be tough (mentally and physically); girls are thought to be softer and it is more acceptable for them to cry or to touch each other. Girls walk about arm-in-arm with each other, but boys don't.

Often, boys do things with their fathers. They play or watch football together, or make models. Girls learn cooking from their mothers, and share an interest in clothes or hairdressing. But many children also enjoy spending time with parents of the opposite sex.

Grandparents

Many new mothers turn to their own mothers or to their sisters for advice and information about bringing up children.

Grandparents, whether they live with the rest of the family or not, usually have a very special role. When a young couple have babies, many grandparents visit, give advice and, above all, give practical help. They help in looking after babies or children. They can act as substitute parents on a temporary basis, giving a rest to the parents. They may do shopping, cooking, or gardening. They may provide financial help, or someone to talk to.

Grandparents are usually extremely proud of their grandchildren. They can enjoy their grandchildren in a

different way from the way they enjoyed their own children. They do not have twenty-four hours a day responsibility for them. So they may spoil their grandchildren a little, and give them special attention.

Grandchildren

A close bond can develop between grandchildren and their grandparents, who become very special to each other. Grandparents can be a source of great support to the young parents, and a calming influence for the whole family.

Grandparents may have different expectations of children's behaviour from that of the parents. They may be either more strict or more lenient. Customs and values can change from one generation to the next.

Elderly grandparents

When grandparents grow old and are less able to look after themselves, gradually family roles are reversed. It is the turn of their children and grandchildren to provide help.

Their adult children (the parents of today's children) sometimes do a lot of visiting and give help with shopping, cooking or washing.

Some old people live alone and manage well. Others live in sheltered housing, old people's homes or hospitals. Others need company or help from their relatives — their own families — and sometimes go to live with them. This can put a great strain on relationships, especially if the elderly become physically frail or mentally confused.

Other members of the family might have to change bedrooms and alter their living conditions. Perhaps meal-times are different, or meals last longer. Perhaps there is less freedom to choose a television programme or to have friends to the house. There may be more time taken up in talking with grandparents, who are interested in what everyone else is doing.

This new social inter-dependence can be enjoyable. But, sadly, some grandparents need more and more physical care, leading to exhaustion for other members of the family. Then the decision has to be taken, whether or not to find a residential home for the elderly dependent relative.

Decisions

When there are two adults in the family, some decisions are made jointly and others by only one of them. Maybe they discuss together, with or without other members of the family, anything that needs a decision. This might be a decision to move house, to buy a car, to get a dog, where to go on holiday, to decorate the living-room, or to get a new cooker or carpet. It might be a decision to visit other relatives, or to go out on Saturday night.

Some decisions have long-term effects, such as where to live, or which school to choose.

Some decisions are big ones and some are small. Maybe one person makes the big decisions and a different person makes the small ones. But which are big and which are small, and who decides which is which?

3. Family Changes

There may be many changes in the people who are in your family, both before and after your birth. There are also changes in the way in which the family works.

There are small changes in roles and responsibilities all the time. These can be caused by children growing older and undertaking more responsibilities within the family. Or they might be temporary changes, perhaps because one parent is ill and unable to do all that he or she normally does. Then another member of the family takes on additional tasks for a short time.

Permanent changes are caused by changes in the membership of the family.

Who belongs to the family?

The members of a family change through births, marriages, divorces and deaths. The family also changes when its members join, or are joined by, other members.

Perhaps you have brothers and sisters, born before or after you. Possibly your parents and you lived for a time (or still live) with one or more grandparents. Some married couples cannot afford — or find — a home of their own. So they start their married life in the home of the parents of one of them. They don't get much privacy in that case, and they probably later find their own home.

The married couple might later change homes again, or several times, especially if one of them gets a job which means a move. But the family is not changed by a change of home.

It may be that a father's employment means that he lives somewhere else for part of the time. He might have to spend some weeks or months on a ship, or on an army posting. A mother might do night duty in a hospital. A child might be at boarding school. Any member of the family might be ill in hospital. A parent might be in prison. But they all continue to be part of the family, and to return home when they can.

A family can be like an accordion, alternately expanding and contracting. It can expand (by births and marriages) and contract (by marriages and deaths). That's curious, that a marriage can affect a family in two opposite ways. A new member joins the family by marrying an existing member. But equally, an existing member of a family can leave it on marriage, by going to live somewhere else and starting a new family.

Children leaving home

When you are older, you are likely to leave your family and start a new family by getting married and having your own children. Do you then belong to two families? For some purposes, the answer is yes.

Life cycle

Family life involves a cycle of birth, marriage and death. We could start by looking at birth, because that is where we all start.

However, it would be sensible to start with marriage, because that marks the start of a new family.

Marriage

Marriage is a legal contract between a man and a woman, for which there is a minimum age of sixteen in Britain. In Britain, about 90 per cent of the population is likely to marry at least once. In at least one marriage in five, the couple have lived together (cohabited) before marriage. The average age at first marriage is 26 years for men and 24 years for women.

Rather more than one half of all weddings is a religious ceremony, and rather less than one half is a civil ceremony (in a Registrar's Office).

A couple who marry when they are in their early twenties have a possible fifty years or so of married life ahead of them. A hundred years ago, a silver wedding (after twenty-five years of marriage) was quite an achievement. Now, not only is there an increase in the number of golden weddings (fifty years) but also of diamond weddings (sixty years).

Remarriage

Increasingly, people are marrying more than once. There are two main reasons. First is the increasing number of divorces which we will look at in the next chapter. Second is the increasing expectation of life. In other words, people are living longer.

One marriage in three is a remarriage for at least one partner; one marriage in eight is a remarriage for both. Most of these remarriages are after divorce. In the last century, remarriage was almost always after being widowed.

No training for marriage

Marriage is the one career for which there is next to no training, and no test of competence. There are almost no courses (except in some churches) which prepare a couple for marriage. They have no tuition in housekeeping, housework or budgeting, or sexual relationships, let alone in what it is like to live with someone else, morning, noon and night. Books are available on these subjects, but most people follow the lessons learned from their own parents, which are often not enough.

What couples expect from marriage

Nowadays people expect more from marriage than they used to do. They have hopes of love, security, independence, romance, freedom, excitement and enjoyment.

No longer does a man expect to divide his life into

marriage and home (shared with his wife) and work and hobbies (shared with his mates) The two halves are usually mixed and shared.

No longer does a wife expect to give up her job in order to devote her life to housekeeping and having children. Increasingly, wives either return to employment after, or between, the births of their children; or they do not give up employment on marriage, but take maternity leave for each birth.

Many working wives work part-time, so that they still have time to run their homes. By working outside the home, they bring in extra money, they meet other people and they have more to talk about. They can be more interesting to live with than if they have a purely domestic life. A wife who started work as a part-time shop assistant when her second child was accepted by a nursery, said 'It was wonderful, to meet the customers and to forget about nappies and cooking for a few hours.'

The disadvantage to wives of working only part-time (or not at all) is that they can lose chances of promotion and of progressing in a career.

So, there we have a newly married couple who have probably set up house on their own, and are quite likely to be thinking of having children.

Birth

Rather more than one couple in ten will have no children. They could be described as a mini-family. Some of them are unable for medical or other reasons to have children, and some of them choose not to have any.

We are more concerned in this book with the vast majority of couples, those who do have children. On average, their first child is born after two and a half years of marriage. Nowadays nearly all British babies are born in hospital, and most fathers are present at the birth. Only two generations ago, many babies were born at home.

Not very long ago, babies were usually fed 'by the clock' — that is, at four hourly intervals. Now, they are more often fed 'on demand' — when they cry from hunger.

The birth of the first child makes a big difference to the parents' lives. They have less freedom, and more domestic work. The mother may feel lonely, as she takes most of the responsibility for looking after a new member of the family.

Maybe three people have to live on one income, instead of two people on two incomes. The parents have a new, ever-present, interest and a new person to get to know. They can share pride in the baby, share some of the caring (bathing and dressing the baby, changing nappies or getting up in the night to a crying baby), and they have a new topic of conversation. The parents will feel that they have become a family.

A family in Britain now has fewer than two children on average. A hundred years ago, a family had an average of five children, but quite a number died when they were very young. Modern mothers are less likely than their great-grandmothers to be tied to an endless progression of pregnancy, childbirth and looking after babies. Mothers now have more freedom to seek employment and to take up interests outside the home.

Adoption

Adoption is similar to birth, in bringing a new child into the family. Therefore it seems sensible to consider adoption at this point.

Some children are adopted by their parents, instead of being born to them. If a couple find that they are unable to have a baby for medical reasons, they are usually very sad. Then they sometimes apply to an adoption agency in the hope that they might find a child who, for some reason, has no home or family.

Other parents might have children born to them but want to increase their family with a child who would otherwise have no family.

Children who are adopted usually had natural parents who were unable to bring them up or provide a home. The alternative, for these children, might have been to live in a children's home. Indeed, some children do spend some months or years in a children's home before being adopted.

Children who are adopted can be sure that they were very much wanted by their adoptive parents. Even so, they often want some information about their original parents. If they do, they are allowed to have this when they reach the age of eighteen.

For instance, Sally had always known she was adopted but she had often wondered what her natural mother was like, and how she had felt about giving up her baby. Sally was helped to get in touch with her mother. They were a little shy together at first, but were soon firm friends. Now, they meet only occasionally, but each is happier to know something about how the other is getting on.

There used to be many more children available for adoption than there are now. The chief reason is that unmarried mothers are more likely to be able to keep their babies.

At one time, most adoptions were of small babies. Now, some couples adopt older children. Many couples who want to adopt are unable to do so now, because there are no children available to match up with them.

If you want to read more about adoption, have a look at a book called *So You're Adopted* by James Stanford.

Fostering

Some couples, with or without children of their own, become registered foster-parents. They offer a home to children whose parents are, perhaps temporarily, unable to care for them. Fostering can be short-term, maybe for a few days or weeks in an emergency, or long-term for children who have no other home but are not likely to be adopted.

Babies or children who are waiting to be adopted often spend a little time with foster-parents until a permanent home has been arranged for them.

Fostering provides a temporary home with security and the experience of life in a caring family. Families who have foster-children may have many changes and can gain as well as give love.

Death

The third stage in the life cycle is death. The main causes of death are heart disease (especially for men) and cancer (especially for women). Modern medicine and surgery keep alive many people who would have died in the past.

In the last 80 years, there has been a great increase in how long people can expect to live. In 1901, a boy was likely to live to the age of 48 and a girl to 52. By 1981, these figures had changed to 70 and 76. Those averages hide the fact that an increasing number of people now live to over 80.

Death in the family

The death of any member of a family comes as a shock to the other members, whether or not it was expected. Death can come after a short or a long illness or it can be the result of an accident. It can be very sudden and totally unexpected, or it can be seen to be coming.

We will all die one day, but most people don't like to think about their own death or about the death of other members of the family. And we don't talk much about death, so that we often have difficulties in coping with our feelings when someone dies.

Death comes most often in old age, so grandparents are likely to die before parents, and parents before their children.

The death of a young person, or a child or a baby (before or after birth) can bring strong feelings of shock, loss and disbelief.

After a death

After someone in the family has died, the other members of the family can comfort each other. Sometimes, though, they have difficulty in talking to each other. Then, instead of bottling up their feelings, they can be helped by talking to someone outside the family. It is important for other people to be willing to talk about the dead person, and not to be embarrassed.

Also, after a death, roles will change. There needs to be a redistribution of responsibilities within the family. The dead person's responsibilities have to be taken on by someone else. At the same time, surviving members of the family no longer have the responsibility of caring for the person who has died.

Other family changes

Births, marriages and deaths are visible changes, and all have to be registered. There are other events which lead to big changes in a family.

Starting school

For instance, when a child starts school (or nursery) the mother's day is suddenly quite different. She has to take and fetch the child at fixed times in the day, but she no longer has the care of the child between those times. When her youngest child starts school there is a very big change for a mother, who might feel a sense of loss or of freedom.

Leaving home

When a child leaves home and goes to live somewhere else (for instance, boarding school or college, for employment, travel, marriage or for any other reason) the house is emptier and quieter. There is probably less work but less company. Some parents feel very bereft and sad, when their children leave home. Others welcome the opportunity to plan their lives in a new way.

Illness

The start of a serious illness or handicap in any member of the family can cause a crisis. The future needs to be replanned, especially if somebody is permanently disabled and in need of a lot of care. Sometimes one member of the family will give up a paid job in order to look after another member.

Unemployment

Loss of employment brings great changes to a family. Everyone has to establish a new routine and perhaps redistribute responsibilities. They will probably be worse off financially. One-fifth of British children are in families living below what is called the poverty line, usually because their parents are unemployed. An older child might even give up education after sixteen, in order to start earning for the family, but this is usually a mistake in the long run.

Retirement

Retirement brings less uncertainty and worry than does unemployment. But it is very important for people to prepare themselves for retirement. That includes the wife or husband of the person who is retiring.

People normally retire at the age of 60 or 65. They are usually healthy and active and want to continue with some kind of occupation. This can be a hobby, sport, voluntary work or new paid employment. It is important for their physical and mental health that they have plenty of interesting things to do.

4. One-Parent Families

Families where only one parent lives with the children, and only one parent has the responsibility for the day-to-day care of the children, are usually called one-parent (or single parent) families. This is a useful description, which we will use in this chapter, but it is not strictly accurate. Most so-called one-parent families have two parents, but they do not live together.

There are probably several children in any school class who live with only one parent.

Numbers of one-parent families

Although 84 per cent of children live with their own two parents, there are a great many children who do not live with both of their parents. About ten per cent of children under five, and twenty per cent of children under sixteen, do not live with their two parents.

There are more one-parent families than there used to be, for several reasons. There are five times more divorces than there were twenty years ago. The proportion of births which are illegitimate has trebled in the past twenty years to 15 per cent, but very few illegitimate babies are now offered for adoption. More often, nowadays, an unmarried mother decides to bring up her own baby. And in many cases, the parents live together but are not married to each other.

About one family in seven is looked after by a single parent. On average, children who live in a one-parent family have five years before the remarriage of the parent with whom they live. This means that many more families than one in seven have had the experience of being a one-parent family. We will discuss what happens to them when one parent remarries, in Chapter 5.

Shared characteristics

One-parent families have some things in common, whatever the reason for the absence of one parent. They are likely to have less income than two-parent families, because there is only one parent to earn, and possibly someone else will have to be paid to take a share of the work.

Most one-parent families have previously had two parents living in the family home — two parents who had shared the roles and responsibilities that were described in Chapter 2.

New responsibilities

When one parent dies, or when one parent leaves home, there are more responsibilities to be shared out among the remaining members of the family. The remaining parent, especially, has far more responsibility. Someone has to undertake the tasks which the absent parent did.

Also, children often have to take on responsibilities at an earlier age. These might include looking after younger children, helping with cooking, housework or shopping or doing odd jobs about the house or garden. Quite often the children give extra care and love to the remaining parent.

In one family, Katie was thirteen when her mother died. Katie then used to go to the supermarket every Saturday morning and do the family's weekly shopping.

At first, her father gave her a list and she stuck to it exactly. Then he began to give her a bit of freedom. She could choose between, say, sausages and fish or cabbage and carrots. She could decide whether to plan homemade puddings or to buy them ready made. She quite enjoyed it and sometimes her friends would help her, but she didn't like having to get up early every Saturday. So she changed her routine, and did the shopping on Friday evenings. Sometimes she left her father to do the shopping, while she got on with cooking a meal.

In another family, David and Tom were five and seven when their father left home and didn't return. The boys missed him a lot, and were rather young to do much to

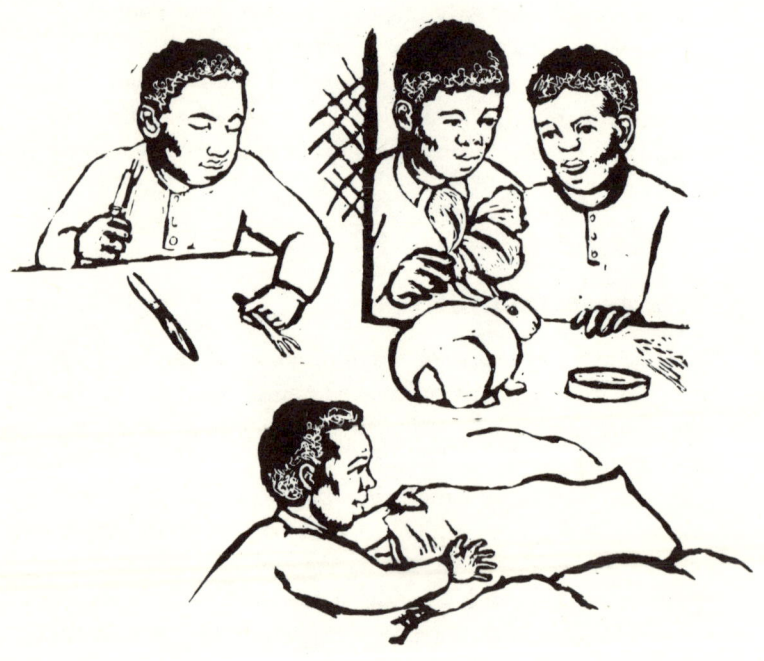

help their mother. But they could see how upset and tired she was. They made a special effort to keep their bedroom tidy, to remember to feed their pet rabbit and to lay the table for meals.

A single parent's part in family life

When there is only one parent, he or she has to take on the role of both parents. A single-parent father has to do more 'mothering' such as cuddling children and looking after their ailments. He has more day-to-day minor crises and gets far more chatter from his children than he used to.

A single-parent mother may have to learn to look after the family's money and do household repairs. She will have to make decisions that her husband used to make. There is no one to share the decisions.

Being a single parent is often very lonely, with no other adult to talk to, to argue with, or to love.

Kinds of one-parent family

There are three kinds of one-parent family. They can be headed by a widowed, a separated or divorced, or an unmarried parent. Most single parents are mothers, but about 11 per cent of one-parent families are looked after by fathers.

Unmarried mothers

About 16 per cent of one-parent families are headed by unmarried mothers.

There have always been one-parent families where the parents were not married to each other, and the unmarried mother brought up her children without their father.

An unmarried mother often lives with her own parents, so that there are three generations in one household. Possibly, in that case, the grandmother takes at least as much responsibility as the mother for looking after the children.

At one time, there was stigma attached to an unmarried mother. That is, she was described with shame or embarrassment. She might have been pressed to name the father of her child and perhaps to marry him. Some churches refused to baptise a child whose father was not named. The child was called illegitimate, though that is a term which will probably soon be abolished.

Nowadays, there is much less criticism of an unmarried mother, and fewer questions are asked. She may live with the child's father without marrying him. This could be because they have chosen not to marry, or because one of them is already married to someone else, and not yet divorced.

Widowed parents

A hundred years ago, many children had only one parent because their other parent had died. Now, that happens far less often, because parents live longer.

About 13 per cent of one-parent families are now headed by widowed mothers. And in some of the 11 per cent headed by single fathers, the fathers are widowed.

Nowadays, few children lose a parent by death. Everyone feels sympathetic if they do, and is sorry for the child. But some people feel too embarrassed to talk about the death, even if the child finds it difficult to think about anything else.

Clearly, there is no choice about which parent the children will live with, when one parent dies. But it is important that children should be told the truth. Sometimes the surviving parent is too upset to explain to children that the other parent will never return. Then, children can be left with false hopes, perhaps that a parent will return from hospital. That will make it far more difficult for them to understand why there are changes at home.

What sort of changes are there? First and most important is the absence of a husband or wife and parent. That means the loss of love and companionship. Secondly, there are practical changes in daily living, which will be similar to those in separated or divorced families.

Separation and divorce

Many children live with only one parent because their parents have split up, and are either separated or divorced. The children still have two parents who live in different homes, and sometimes in different towns (or even different countries). In about 60 per cent of one-parent families, the parents are separated or divorced.

Why do parents split up?

There is seldom one reason for the ending of a marriage, although it may appear to outsiders that it was because of drink, or violence, or that one parent decided to live with a new partner, or some other reason.

Usually a marriage breaks down from a mixture of factors. Maybe the husband and wife begin to have different interests. They spend less and less time together. They each get resentful and irritable. They argue a lot, or else they don't speak to each other. They disagree about money, about bringing up children, about what to do at weekends or about anything or nothing. In anger, perhaps the husband is violent to his wife. In frustration, the wife goes out with another man.

Maybe it is not like that. Some husbands and wives grow apart from each other gradually. Sometimes one partner does not realise that the other one wants to end the marriage.

Planning the separation

In some marriages the separation is planned by the couple. In some, one partner plans it. Sometimes it seems to happen out of the blue. People outside the family are sometimes astonished to hear of the separation, but sometimes they have expected it.

Whatever the reason, everything can build up to the point where one parent decides to leave home, or asks the other one to leave. It was not particularly the fault of either of them. And it was certainly not the fault of their children. Sometimes young children believe that they are to blame when one parent leaves home, but that is not so. The parents separated because they couldn't continue to live with each other.

Parents after separation

After parents have split up, both parents are still responsible for the children, but only one is on the spot. The parent who has the daily care of the children has to take on the role of the absent parent as well, in day-to-day living. This is difficult and can lead to exhaustion and irritability. The other parent can find it difficult to feel responsible, when not living with the children.

The process of separation can be a time of difficult re-adjustment for all members of the family. Sometimes the parents remain good friends; sometimes they feel bitter towards each other.

What is divorce?

Divorce marks the legal ending of a marriage partnership, but it does not affect the relationship between the children and each parent — or it ought not to do so. The parents are still, and will always be, father and mother to their children. Divorce usually happens a year or two after separation.

Divorce is the public acknowledgement that the parents' marriage has ended. For the children, and sometimes for the parents, the earlier separation is more upsetting.

Divorce law

Divorce law in Britain has changed several times in recent years, and divorce can now be granted by the courts for 'irretrievable breakdown' of marriage. This is sometimes described as 'no-fault divorce', although it is still necessary to prove that the marriage has broken down. The evidence required is one of the following:

— the couple have lived apart for two years and both want divorce

— one of them has committed adultery (ie had sexual intercourse with someone else)

— one of them has behaved unreasonably to the other

— one of them has deserted the other for at least two years

— they have lived apart for five years (even though one does not want divorce).

Facts and figures

There has been a huge increase in the number of divorces in recent years. There are now five times as many divorces every year as there were 20 years ago.

One marriage in three is likely to end in divorce. Rather more than half of divorces are between couples who have children. One child in five is likely to have divorced parents before reaching the age of sixteen.

On the other hand, two marriages in three are likely to survive, and four children out of five will not have divorced parents.

The great increase in divorce has been because:

— divorce has become easier to obtain

— there is now less stigma attached to divorce

— divorcing couples are often eligible for free, or cheap, legal services

— the government provides some financial help for one-parent families.

Custody of children

We usually say that the parent with whom the children live has custody of the children.

In the nineteenth century, divorce was rare. When it did happen, children were usually regarded as the father's property and he was awarded custody. At the beginning of the twentieth century, the importance of mother-love became more accepted. As a result, more and more children lived with their mothers after divorce. Now, in roughly 85 per cent of divorced families, the children live with their mother and in 15 per cent with their father.

Children's feelings

Whatever way it happens, children are often shocked and unhappy when their parents separate. Philip said, 'I knew my parents argued a lot, but I never expected them to split up.' Marion said she hadn't even known her parents were unhappy. She said, 'I thought we were a happy family. Why did they have to split up? They never told me they weren't getting on.'

Parents are often so busy dealing with their own feelings and with the practicalities of separation, that they are unable to notice their children's feelings.

Children are likely to feel a mixture of anger, sadness, worry, surprise and possibly relief. It is perfectly normal to have all these feelings and to feel a bit mixed up. It is often comforting to talk to others in the same situation.

Changes for children

After their parents split up, children are likely to:

— live in poorer quality housing

— have a lower standard of living

— receive less attention from their parents

— be partly looked after by someone else such as a granny

— be latchkey children (letting themselves into an empty house after school)

— take on more domestic responsibilities

— grow up a little faster.

And possibly:

— there will be several changes of home

— children will live first with one parent, then with the other

— brothers and sisters will be divided

— there will be a step-parent
— there will be different surnames within the family
— there will be stepbrothers and stepsisters
— there will be half-brothers and half-sisters.

For the moment, we will leave aside the subject of stepfamilies. They will be discussed in the next chapter.

Access

Access is the legal word used to describe children visiting, or being visited by, the parent they don't live with.

Between a quarter and a third of children of separated parents lose touch with one parent as an immediate result

of the separation. Within a year or so of separation, about one half lose touch with one parent.

It is important for the children to keep in touch with the absent parent during the difficult time of separation. The absent parent can still be a part-time parent, so that the children have a part-time family as well as the one they live in. They can be part of two different families at the same time.

Often, it is difficult to pick up the threads of an earlier relationship between parent and child, after losing touch. If each parent and the children can continue to show that they love and need each other, future relationships will be much easier. Love between parent and child does not end when parents split up.

At first, it can seem very strange for children to have to arrange to see one parent at a fixed time. Everyone wonders what to do during the afternoon or evening. Gradually, families can settle into whatever arrangements feel comfortable. Parent and children can talk, can share a hobby or a sport, and can catch up on news of what each has been doing. They can go somewhere together, like a museum or a library, go shopping or have a picnic. Or they can stay in the house and enjoy just being together.

If you want to know more about what happens to families whose parents separate and divorce, you could look at a book called *When Parents Split Up*, by Ann Mitchell.

Conclusions

There are some good things about being in a one-parent family. The children usually have an even closer relationship with the remaining parent than they had before.

5. New Families

One-parent families often change yet again, and become two-parent families. Many single parents remarry or cohabit (live together like husband and wife). Some cohabit before getting married. More than half of divorced parents are likely to remarry within five years of divorce.

As far as the family is concerned, the roles and relationships are much the same, whether or not they are married. So, to simplify discussion, we will assume that they are married.

Stepfamilies

These families are described as stepfamilies or, sometimes, reconstituted or blended families.

One of the adults becomes a step-parent to the children of the family, but not a replacement parent. As William said, when his mother remarried, 'You can't just change fathers like that, can you? Mum's new husband is Jim, and he's my step-dad. I've still got my own Dad, though he doesn't live with us.'

It is important to remember that children still have their own two parents, so a step-parent can be welcomed as an extra member of the family (but is sometimes resented).

Myths

There are two myths about step-parents and especially about stepmothers. One is that there will be instant love between the children and their step-parent. That is, that the family will once again be 'normal' with two parents. The other is that of a wicked stepmother who will be unkind to her stepchildren, like Cinderella's stepmother.

These ideas are at opposite extremes. Both are basically false, although there is a bit of truth in each. It is certainly good to have two adults in a family. They can share responsibilities, provide love and companionship for each other, and provide the children with a male and female parent-figure. But step-parenting is not easy. The new relationships need to be worked at.

Parent and step-parent

The parent and step-parent chose to live with each other. So their relationship to each other is much the same as that of the husband and wife described in Chapter 2. The big difference, for them, is that they start their marriage (or partnership) with the children of at least one of them. So they don't have a chance to get to know each other just on their own. The step-parent is plunged into a new life with ready-made children.

A stepfather or stepmother can relieve a parent of responsibilities previously tackled alone. These would include child care, house repairs, domestic tasks and financial affairs. But a step-parent is wise not to be too quick to share the care of stepchildren. They all need to feel their way into new roles and relationships.

Children and step-parents

The children, also, have big changes in their lives when a step-parent joins the family. What sort of changes? First, they have to share the attention of their parent with the step-parent: their own parent has less time for them. There may be less opportunity for private conversations with their own parent. Second, they may have fewer responsibilities because there is an extra adult to take a share.

Some children might be relieved that they have less responsibility and less domestic work. Others might feel annoyed that they have to give up some tasks to the step-parent, or to their own parent who is now less hard-pressed. Maybe they had earlier enjoyed the importance of being the 'man of the house', or staying up late as company for their parent.

The step-parent will need time to discover who does what and when and how. Even if he or she had been a frequent visitor to the house, that is not the same as living there and being part of the family.

Stepfathers and stepmothers

There are differences between the roles of stepfathers and stepmothers. A stepfather may be out all day and not see as much of his stepchildren as a stepmother would.

A stepmother often has more to get used to than a stepfather does. She is likely to be responsible for day-to-day domestic tasks. She can find it difficult to remember that John won't eat bananas or eggs and that Susan hates raw vegetables. She might forget that John has to take his games equipment to school on Wednesdays and Fridays, that Susan has a dancing class after school on Mondays and brings a friend to tea every Friday. She probably doesn't know which of them has already had chicken-pox or how seriously to take complaints of sore throats.

Discipline

It must be difficult for step-parents, especially if they have children of their own, not to lay down rules for their new stepchildren. Dick was rude to his stepmother when she criticised his table manners. 'You can't tell me what to do. You're not my real mother,' he said. 'My real mother never stopped me eating off my knife.' His father might have difficulties in being loyal to his new wife as well as being fair to the children, if he has to act as umpire in arguments.

In another family, Danny said with a sigh of relief, 'My Mum's still the boss.' He had been afraid that his stepfather would start telling him what to do and what time to come home.

Surnames

When a mother remarries she normally changes her surname to that of her new husband. Her children will then have a different surname from their mother. In some families, arrangements are then made for the children to change their surname also. But if they are in touch with their own father, he might quite fairly make objections.

Part-time stepfamilies

We have already seen that children can have two families, one headed by each of their own parents.

When the absent parent (that is, the parent the children do not live with) remarries, the children will have a step-parent in that home. When they visit, and especially if they sleep overnight, they could find some changes. Rooms, furniture, routine might all be different. And the parent they visit would probably want to include the new step-parent in any activities.

More stepchildren

Often a step-parent who joins a family already has children from a previous marriage. Those children are stepchildren to the parent, and stepbrothers and stepsisters to the children in the family. That is so, whether or not the other children come to live in the family.

Half-brothers and half-sisters

If a parent and step-parent have a new baby, the baby is a half-brother or half-sister to the children of each parent. That is because they share one parent. The new baby inherits some characteristics from each parent. So he or she shares some characteristics with the half-brothers and half-sisters.

Other relationships

After a remarriage, there are not only step-parents and stepchildren, but also step-grandparents. Maybe there are also stepcousins, stepaunts and stepuncles. And if an older person becomes a step-parent on marriage, he or she might become an instant step-grandparent as well.

Step-relationships can be extremely complicated!

6. Other Families

There are too many variations on family life to be able to consider them all in this book.

In some places in Britain, there are groups of people whose families originally came from other countries. The largest numbers are Indian, Pakistani, West Indian and Chinese. They often keep to the customs and habits of those countries, even when they live and work or go to school with people whose families have always lived in Britain.

One example is the duty felt by families in Britain to send money to their relatives in their own countries. Family members often work long hours in order to support their distant relatives.

In some groups, the father is head of the family in every way: he controls its money and all its activities. In those families, the mothers may spend most of their day at home and not meet many other people.

In some Asian groups, the girls and women have little social freedom to mix with other people. Their rules of behaviour are more strict than those of modern British families, where young people question what their parents do and say. There are advantages and disadvantages in both ways of life.

Another example of different family life is that of marriages arranged through parents of young people who have never met each other. These marriages can be very successful if the parents have carefully chosen marriage partners suitable for their sons and daughters. In India, marriages sometimes take place between young children who each continue to live with their own parents for several more years.

In other countries, 'family' might mean something different from the descriptions in this book. For example, in some parts of Africa, a wife lives with all of her female relations who help in looking after each other's children.

In Israel, children from several families are sometimes looked after communally in a kibbutz: but recently parents have been much more involved in helping to look after their own children.

In some Moslem countries, a man can have more than one wife.

You might find it interesting to find out more about other kinds of family, perhaps from others in your class, and to compare their customs with your own.